THANK YOU

Thank you for purchasing "No Pun Intended Too"!
We hope you enjoy this collection of
witty, pun-filled jokes

Your support means the world to us, and we're grateful you chose our joke book to tickle your funny bone.

As an independent publishing company, we rely on feedback from readers like you to help us grow and improve our offerings. If you could take a moment to leave a review on Amazon, it would be a huge help to us. Your review will provide valuable insight for potential readers and help our little book of laughs reach a wider audience.

Please consider leaving a review

Scan The QR Code to Review

WILL LIVINGTON© COPYRIGHT 2023

SIGN UP TO OUR LIST AND GET FREE STUFF!

Scan the QR code & sign up for our email list and we will send you 10 Free coloring pages from our latest book release.
Go To:

https://subscribepage.io/SketchSiren

WHAT DO MUMMIES LISTEN TO ON HALLOWEEN?

Wrap music

WHERE DOES DRACULA KEEP HIS MONEY?

In a blood bank

I LIKE A WOMAN WITH A HEAD ON HER SHOULDERS

I hate necks

TWO FISH IN A TANK. ONE SAYS:

'How do you drive this thing?

IT DOESN'T MATTER HOW MUCH YOU PUSH THE ENVELOPE.

It'll still be stationary

WHAT DID THE CONFEDERATE SOLDIERS USE TO EAT OFF OF?

Civil ware

I WALKED INTO MY SISTER'S ROOM AND TRIPPED ON A BRA.

It was a booby-trap

A BOOK JUST FELL ON MY HEAD..

only have my shelf to blame

WHAT IS THE LEADING CAUSE OF DIVORCE IN LONG-TERM MARRIAGES?

A stalemate

BAKERS TRADE BREAD RECIPES..

but only on a knead
to know basis

A MOON ROCK TASTES BETTER THAN AN EARTHLY ROCK

because it's meteor.

A BACKWARDS POET

Writes inverse

I USED TO BE ADDICTED TO SOAP

but I'm clean now

DID YOU KNOW 3.14% OF SAILORS

Arrr pi rates

I STAYED UP ALL NIGHT WONDERING WHERE THE SUN WENT.

Then it dawned on me

WHAT DID THE MERMAID WEAR TO HER MATH CLASS?

An algae bra.

WHY DID THE SCARECROW GET A PROMOTION?

He was outstanding in his field.

MONEY TALKS

but all mine ever says is goodbye

I TRIED TO CATCH SOME FOG EARLIER.

I mist

YOU KNOW WHAT'S NOT RIGHT?

Left..

WHAT DOES A PIRATE SAY WHILE EATING SUSHI?

Ahoy! Pass me some soy

YOU WANNA HEAR A JOKE ABOUT PIZZA?

Never mind its too cheesy

IF A DISH TOWEL COULD TELL A JOKE

I sink it would have a sense of humor

WHAT DID THE GREEN GRAPE SAY TO THE PURPLE GRAPE?

Breathe you idiot!

WHY CAN'T A NOSE BE 12 INCHES?

Because than it would be a foot

A BOILED EGG IN THE MORNING

is really hard to beat

I'M READING A BOOK ABOUT ANTI-GRAVITY.

Its really hard to put down

I'M GLAD I KNOW SIGN LANGUAGE

It's become quite handy.

I FORGOT HOW TO THROW A BOOMERANG.

But it came back to me.

WHEN A CLOCK IS HUNGRY...

it goes back four seconds

ONCE HEARD A JOKE ABOUT AMNESIA...

But I fogot how it goes

WHEN THE POWER WENT OUT AT THE SCHOOL...

The children... were de-lighted

THERE WAS ONCE A CROSSED-EYED TEACHER...

who had issues controlling his pupils

DIARRHEA IS HEREDITARY...

It runs in your jeans

WHAT IS A PIRATE'S FAVORITE LETTER?

'Tis the C.

THOSE TWO MEN DRINKING BATTERY ACID

will soon be charged.

THE DWARF PSYCHIC ESCAPED PRISON.

He was a small medium at large

I'M INCLINED...

To be laid back

THE NEWSPAPER HEADLINE READS:

Cartoonist found dead at home, details are sketchy

THE MAGICIAN GOT FRUSTRATED

and pulled out his hare

A CRIMINAL'S BEST ASSET...

is his lie-ability

I HEARD ABOUT THE GUY WHO GOT HIT IN THE HEAD WITH A CAN OF SODA

He is lucky it was a soft drink.

WHAT DID THE TRIANGLE SAY TO THE CIRCLE?

You're so pointless

WHAT DID THE CANNIBAL GET WHEN HE SHOWED UP TO THE PARTY LATE?

A cold shoulder!

WHY DID THE COFFEE FILE A POLICE REPORT?

It got mugged!

WHY DID THE BAKER GO TO THERAPY?

He kneaded it!

WHY DID THE EGG GO TO SCHOOL?

To get a little more egg-ucated!

WHY DID THE CLOCK GO TO THE DOCTOR?

It was having a tough time!

WHY DON'T SPAGHETTI AND MACARONI LIKE EACH OTHER?

They dont have a pasta-tive relationship!

WHY DID THE BANKER SWITCH CAREERS?

He lost interest!

WHAT DO YOU CALL CHEESE THAT ISN'T YOURS?

Nacho cheese

WHY WAS THE ANT SO CONFUSED?

All its uncles were ants too!

WHY WAS THE MATH BOOK UNHAPPY?

It had so many problems!

WHY DID THE PICTURE GO TO JAIL?

It was framed!

HOW DOES A CAT BECOME A MILLIONAIRE?

It starts with a purrfect investment!

WHAT DO YOU GET WHEN YOU CROSS A DOG AND A COMPUTER?

Lots of bytes!

WHY DO TREES HAVE MULTIPLE JOBS?

Because they're really good at branching out!

WHY DID THE COW GO TO OUTER SPACE?

To see the moooo-n

WHAT DO YOU GET WHEN YOU CROSS A FISH AND A BANKER?

A loan shark!

WHY DON'T SCIENTISTS TRUST ATOMS?

They make up everything!

WHY DID THE CHICKEN GO TO JAIL?

For using fowl language!

WHY DID THE ICE CREAM GET A BAD REPORT CARD?

It kept freezing during tests!

WHY DID THE TOMATO TURN RED?

It saw the salad dressing!

WHAT'S A DOG'S FAVORITE TYPE OF HOUSE?

Any woof over its head will do!

WHAT'S A GHOST'S FAVORITE DESSERT?

Boo-berry pie!

WHAT DID THE OCEAN SAY TO THE SHORE?

Nothing it just waved

WHY DID THE ELEPHANT BRING A SUITCASE TO THE ZOO?

Everything wouldn't fit in his trunk!

WHY DON'T ALLIGATORS LIKE FAST FOOD?

Because they can't catch it!

WHY DON'T OYSTERS DONATE TO CHARITY?

They're very shellfish!

WHY DO SEAGULLS FLY OVER THE SEA?

Because if they flew over the bay, they'd be bagels!

WHAT DO BEES USE TO STYLE THEIR HAIR?

Honeycombs!

WHY DID THE LION BECOME A GARDENER?

He wanted to cultivate his pride!

WHAT DO FROGS DO WITH PAPER?

Rip-it!

WHY DID THE LEAF GO TO THE DOCTOR?

It was feeling a little green!

WHAT'S A STRAWBERRY'S FAVORITE DANCE MOVE?

The jam!

WHY DON'T PENGUINS LIKE TALKING TO STRANGERS AT PARTIES?

They find it hard to break the ice!

WHY DID THE SQUIRREL TAKE UP ACTING?

It had a nutty personality!

WHY ARE RABBITS SO GOOD AT MATH?

They multiply quickly!

WHY DO WE NEVER TELL SECRETS ON A FARM?

Because the potatoes have eyes and the corn has ears!

WHAT DO YOU CALL A ROW OF RABBITS WALKING BACKWARD?

A receding hare line.

WHY DID THE DUCK BECOME A DETECTIVE?

To quack the case!

WHY DID THE MUSICIAN GO TO JAIL?

He was in treble!

WHY DID THE PLANT BECOME A COMEDIAN?

It had great thyme-ing!

WHY DID THE GOLFER WEAR TWO PAIRS OF PANTS?

In case he got a hole in one!

I USED TO PLAY PIANO BY EAR

But now I use my hands

WHY WAS THE BELT ARRESTED?

It was got caught holding up
a pair of pants.

I ONCE TOLD A CHEMISTRY JOKE

But it had no reaction

I USED TO BE A BAKER

But I couldn't make enough dough

MY MATH TEACHER CALLED ME AVERAGE.

How mean

WHAT DO YOU CALL A PILE OF CATS?

A meowtain!

I WAS STRUGGLING TO FIGURE OUT HOW LIGHTNING WORKS

But then it struck me!

WOMEN SHOULD NOT HAVE CHILDREN AFTER 35

Really, 35 children are enough

WHY DID THE ORANGE STOP ROLLING DOWN THE HILL?

It ran out of juice

WHY DID THE BICYCLE FALL OVER?

It was two tired

I'M FRIENDS WITH ALL THE ELECTRICIANS IN MY TOWN.

I'm always looking for new connections

WHY DON'T SOME COUPLES GO TO THE GYM?

Because some relationships don't workout.

I ONCE ATE A WATCH...

It was time consuming

WHAT DO YOU CALL A DINOSAUR WITH AN EXTENSIVE VOCABULARY?

A thesaurus-rex!

WHY DID THE COFFEE BEAN GIVE A STANDING OVATION?

the show was grounds for applause!

WHY DO COWS HAVE HOOVES INSTEAD OF FEET?

Because they lactose!

HOW DOES A COMPUTER GET DRUNK?

It takes screenshots.

I'D TELL YOU A JOKE ABOUT A BED

but it hasn't been made up yet.

WHAT DO YOU CALL A FAKE NOODLE?

An impasta!

WHAT DO YOU CALL A CAN OPENER THAT DOESN'T WORK?

A can't opener

WHY DID THE SCARECROW BECOME A MUSICIAN?

He had great hay-rmony.

WHY DID THE BICYCLE GO TO THERAPY?

It couldn't stand up for itself.

WHAT DO YOU CALL A BEE THAT CAN'T MAKE UP ITS MIND?

A maybe!

WHY DID THE MUSHROOM GO TO THE PARTY?

Because it was a fungi.

WHAT DO YOU CALL A SINGING COMPUTER?

A-Dell

ALWAYS BORROW MONEY FROM A PESSIMIST

He won't
expect it back.

WHY COULDN'T THE BICYCLE FIND ITS WAY HOME?

It lost its bearings.

MY FIRST EXPERIENCE WITH CULTURE SHOCK

Was probably when I peed
on an electric fence

WHAT DO YOU GET WHEN YOU CROSS A SNOWMAN AND A VAMPIRE?

Frostbite!

I HAVE A LOT OF GROWING UP TO DO

I realized that the other day in my fort

I USED TO BE INDECISIVE

Now I'm not sure

WHAT DO YOU CALL A BEAR WITH NO TEETH?

A gummy bear

WHY DID THE TREE GO TO THE BARBER?

It needed a trim

WHY DID THE TEACHER GO TO THE BEACH?

To test the waters

WHY DO FISH LIVE IN SALTWATER?

Because pepper water would make them sneeze.

WHY DID THE SCARECROW BECOME A SPY?

He could blend in with any crowd.

WHY DID THE TOILET PAPER ROLL DOWN THE HILL?

To get to the bottom.

WHY WAS THE BROOM LATE FOR WORK?

It overswept!

WHY DID THE SCARECROW BECOME A SCIENTIST?

He was great at field research.

WHAT DO YOU CALL A GROUP OF MUSICAL CATS?

A meow-semble!

WHY DID THE SCARECROW BECOME A DANCER?

He had great rhythm in his straw.

I'D TELL YOU A JOKE ABOUT A CEILING

but it's way over your head.

BOSS TOLD ME TO HAVE A GOOD DAY

So I went home

WHAT DO YOU CALL A SNOBBISH CRIMINAL GOING DOWNSTAIRS?

A condescending con descending!

DID YOU HEAR ABOUT THE GUY WHO CUT OFF THE LEFT SIDE OF HIS BODY?

He's all right now

I DON'T PLAY SOCCER BECAUSE I ENJOY THE SPORT.

I'm just doing it for kicks!

WHY DO CHICKEN COOPS ONLY HAVE TWO DOORS?

Because if they had four, they'd be chicken sedans!

DID YOU HEAR ABOUT THE KIDNAPPING AT THE PLAYGROUND?

He's ok. He woke up!

I WOULD TELL YOU A JOKE ABOUT A BROKEN ELEVATOR

But it's not an uplifting joke.

I USE TO HATE FACIAL HAIR

but then it grew on me.

I WOULD TELL YOU A JOKE ABOUT CONSTRUCTION..

but I'm still working on it.

HOW DO YOU THROW A SPACE PARTY?

You just planet!

WHY DID THE IRON BECOME A COMEDIAN?

It had impressive humor!

WHY DID THE KING GO TO THE DENTIST?

To get his royal crown fixed!

WHY DID THE GEOLOGIST GO TO THERAPY?

He had too many unresolved layers!

WHY WAS THE CANDY WRAPPER ARRESTED?

It was caught in a sticky situation!

WHY DON'T SKELETONS FIGHT EACH OTHER?

Because they have no guts

WHY DID THE FIREFIGHTER BECOME A BAKER?

He knew how to handle the heat!

WHY DID THE PEANUT START TELLING JOKES?

It wanted to be a-shell-e-brity!

WHAT DID THE GRAPE SAY WHEN IT GOT STEPPED ON?

Nothing, it just let out a little wine!

WHY DID THE TEAPOT GO TO THERAPY?

It had a lot of emotional tea baggage!

WHY WAS THE SODA SO FRIENDLY?

It bubbly personality

WHAT DID THE BUDDHIST SAY TO THE HOT DOG VENDOR?

Make me one with everything.

WHY DID THE HIPSTER BURN HIS MOUTH?

He drank the coffee before it was cool.

WHY DID THE NURSE NEED A RED PEN?

In case she needed to draw blood.

I POURED ROOT BEER IN A SQUARE GLASS.

Now I just have beer

HOW DOES A RABBI MAKE COFFEE?

Hebrews it

WHY CAN'T MALE ANTS SINK?

They're buoy-ant.

WHAT IS AN ASTRONAUT'S FAVORITE PART ON A COMPUTER?

The spacebar

DID YOU HEAR ABOUT THE MATHEMATICIAN WHO'S AFRAID OF NEGATIVE NUMBERS?

He'll stop at nothing to avoid them

WHAT DID 0 SAY TO 8?

Nice belt

WHAT KIND OF EXERCISE DO LAZY PEOPLE DO?

Diddly-squats.

WHAT'S A PRIVATE INVESTIGATOR'S FAVORITE SHOE?

Sneak-ers

WHAT DO YOU CALL A PONY WITH A COUGH?

A little horse

WHY AREN'T KOALAS ACTUAL BEARS?

They don't meet the koalafications

WHY COULDN'T THE LEOPARD PLAY HIDE-AND-SEEK?

Because he was always spotted

HOW DO YOU MAKE A TISSUE DANCE?

You put a little boogie in it

WHY DID THE CHICKEN CROSS THE PLAYGROUND?

To get to the other slide

WHY DID THE TEDDY BEAR SAY NO TO DESSERT?

Because she was stuffed

WHAT DID ONE TRAFFIC LIGHT SAY TO THE OTHER?

Stop looking at me, I'm changing

WHAT DO YOU CALL BEARS WITH NO EARS?

B

WHAT'S A SNAKE'S FAVORITE SUBJECT IN SCHOOL?

Hiss-tory

WHAT'S A FOOT LONG AND SLIPPERY?

A slipper

WHAT IS STICKY AND BROWN?

A stick

WHAT DID THE LEFT EYE SAY TO THE RIGHT EYE?

Between us, something smells

WHY WON'T PEANUT BUTTER TELL YOU A SECRET?

He's afraid you'll spread it

WHY DID THE GYM CLOSE DOWN?

It just didn't work out

WHY DO BIRDS FLY SOUTH IN THE WINTER?

It's faster then walking

TWO ARTISTS HAD AN ART CONTEST.

It ended in a draw

WHAT'S A CAT'S FAVORITE DESSERT?

A bowl full of mice-cream

WHAT DO YOU CALL A BOOMERANG THAT DOESN'T COME BACK?

A stick

WHAT ARE A SHARK'S TWO FAVORITE WORDS?

Man overboard

WHAT DO YOU CALL A TRAIN CARRYING BUBBLEGUM?

A chew-chew train

WHAT DO YOU CALL A MAGIC DOG?

A labracadabrador

WHY ARE GHOSTS SUCH BAD LIARS?

Because you can see right through them

WHAT DID THE BUFFALO SAY WHEN HIS SON LEFT FOR COLLEGE?

Bison

DESPITE THE HIGH COST OF LIVING

It still remains popular

TWO WIFI ENGINEERS GOT MARRIED

The reception was fantastic

THE FUTURE, THE PRESENT, AND THE PAST WALK INTO A BAR

Things got a little tense

I DON'T SUFFER FROM INSANITY

I enjoy every minute of it

WHERE DO FISH SLEEP?

In a riverbed

R.I.P. BOILING WATER?

You will be mist

SPRING IS HERE!

I got so excited I wet my plants

WHY DID THE CLOCK GET KICKED OUT OF THE LIBRARY?

It tocked too much

I HAD A DREAM ABOUT BEING A MUFFLER.

I woke up exhausted

WHY WAS THE COMPUTER ALWAYS AT THE BEACH?

It just loved surfing

WHY WAS THE MATH PROBLEM SO UNHAPPY?

It had too many variables

WHY DID THE SCARECROW BECOME A CHEF?

He knew how to make amazing field-to-table dishes.

WHY WAS THE COMPUTER COLD?

It left its Windows open

WHAT DO YOU CALL A SNOWMAN WITH A SIX-PACK?

An abdominal snowman

WHY DID THE SCARECROW BECOME A DETECTIVE?

He was great at finding needles in haystacks

WHAT DINOSAUR NEVER GIVES UP?

A try-ceratops

WHAT DO YOU CALL A SHOE MADE OUT OF A BANANA?

A slipper

WHAT'S FORREST GUMP'S FACEBOOK PASSWORD?

1Forest1

WHAT DOES A BABY COMPUTER CALL HIS FATHER

Data

WHAT DO YOU CALL A COW THAT PLAYS THE GUITAR?

A moo-sician

WHAT DID ONE PLATE SAY TO HIS FRIEND?

Tonight, dinner is on me.

I TRIED TO SUE THE AIRPORT FOR MISPLACING MY LUGGAGE

I lost my case

WHY DOESN'T THE SUN GO TO COLLEGE?

Because it already has a million degrees.

WHY DID THE BANANA GO TO THE DOCTOR?

Because it wasn't peeling well!

DID YOU HEAR ABOUT THE CIRCUS FIRE?

It was in tents

WHAT DO YOU CALL AN ALLIGATOR THAT WEARS A VEST AND A BOWTIE?

An investi-gator

WHAT DID THE ZOMBIE SAY TO HIS DATE?

I just love a woman with brains

WHY DON'T CATS PLAY POKER IN THE JUNGLE?

Too many cheetahs!

WHAT DO YOU CALL A LAZY KANGAROO?

A pouch potato!

WHY DID THE BEAR BREAK UP WITH HIS GIRLFRIEND?

She was unbearable!

WHY DID THE ZOMBIE GO TO THE DOCTOR?

It had a cough-in its throat!

WHAT'S A ZOMBIE'S FAVORITE CEREAL?

Rice Creepies!

CAN FEBRUARY MARCH?

No, but April May

WHAT DO YOU CALL A SLEEPING BULL?

A bulldozer!

HOW DO YOU CATCH A SQUIRREL?

Climb up a tree and act like a nut!

WHY DON'T ZOMBIES EAT CLOWNS?

They taste funny

WHAT DO YOU CALL A PIG THAT DOES KARATE?

A pork chop!

WHAT TIME DID THE MAN GO TO THE DENTIST?

Tooth-hurty

WHY DID THE ASTRONAUT BREAK UP WITH HIS GIRLFRIEND?

He needed more space!

WHAT DO YOU CALL A FISH WEARING A BOW TIE?

Sofishticated

WHERE DO YOU LEARN TO MAKE A BANANA SPLIT?

Sundae school

WHY DO ELEPHANTS NEVER USE COMPUTERS?

They're afraid of mice!

WHY DID THE SNAIL PAINT AN "S" ON HIS CAR?

So when it drove by,
people would say "Look at that S-car go!"

HOW DOES A PENGUIN BUILD ITS HOUSE?

Igloos it together!

WHY DID THE CAR BREAK UP WITH HIS GIRLFRIEND?

She was always driving him crazy!

WHY DID THE COOKIE GO TO THE DOCTOR?

Because it felt crummy!

WHAT DO YOU CALL A CAR THAT'S FULL OF RABBITS?

A bunny-hopper!

WHY DID THE MECHANIC SLEEP UNDER THE CAR?

To wake up oily in the morning!

WHAT DO YOU CALL AN AVOCADO THAT'S BEEN BLESSED BY A PRIEST?

Holy Guacamole!

WHAT DID TENNESSEE?

The same thing as Arkansas

WHAT DID THE NOSE TELL THE FINGER?

Stop picking on me!

TRYING TO WRITE WITH A BROKEN PENCIL

Is pointless

MY COMPUTER'S GOT THE MILEY VIRUS.

It's stopped twerking

A BOOK JUST FELL ON MY HEAD

I've only got myshelf to blame

I WASN'T ORIGINALLY GOING TO GET A BRAIN TRANSPLANT

but then I changed my mind

I HAD A JOB TYING SAUSAGES TOGETHER,

but I couldn't make ends meet

A FRIEND OF MINE TRIED TO ANNOY ME WITH BIRD PUNS

but toucan play at that game

I WONDERED WHY THE FRISBEE WAS GETTING BIGGER

Then it hit me

A COURTROOM ARTIST WAS ARRESTED TODAY

The details are sketchy

WANT TO HEAR A JOKE ABOUT PAPER?

Never mind, it's tearable

DID YOU HEAR ABOUT THE PESSIMIST WHO HATES GERMAN SAUSAGE?

He always fears the Wurst

I'VE WRITTEN A SONG ABOUT TORTILLAS

Actually, it's more of a wrap

LONG FAIRY TALES HAVE A TENDENCY

to dragon

I WAS GOING TO SHARE A VEGETABLE JOKE

But it's corny

TWO CHEESE TRUCKS RAN INTO EACH OTHER

De-brie was everywhere

I LOVE GIANT SQUID JOKES

They're always kraken me up!

I FOUND A ROCK WHICH MEASURED 1760 YARDS IN LENGTH

Must be some kind of milestone

I MET THE MAN WHO INVENTED THE WINDOWSILL

He's a ledge and..

MY EX USED TO HIT ME WITH STRINGED INSTRUMENTS

She had a history of violins

I WAS HOPING TO STEAL SOME LEFTOVERS FROM THE PARTY

but my plans were foiled

SIMBA WAS WALKING SO SLOWLY

I told him to Mufasa

MOST PEOPLE ARE SHOCKED WHEN THEY FIND OUT

how bad an electrician I am

I LOST MY MOOD RING THE OTHER DAY

I'm not sure how to feel about it

SOME CLOWN OPENED THE DOOR FOR ME THIS MORNING

That was a nice jester

I DON'T TRUST STAIRCASES

They're always up to something

WHY ARE SKELETONS SO CALM?

Because nothing gets under their skin

THE FIRST TIME I GOT A UNIVERSAL REMOTE CONTROL

I thought, "this changes everything"

I GOT FIRED FROM THE CANDLE FACTORY BECAUSE

I refused to work wick ends

I'M VERY PLEASED WITH MY NEW FRIDGE MAGNET

So far I've got twelve fridges

I NEED TO STOP DRINKING SO MUCH MILK

It's an udder disgrace

WHY DID THE CAN CRUSHER QUIT HIS JOB?

Because it was soda pressing

DID YOU HEAR ABOUT THE GUY WHO STOLE A CALENDAR?

He got twelve months!

MY FRIEND IS A BAKER WHO MOONLIGHTS AS A BOXER

He really knows how to roll with the punches!

I QUIT MY JOB AT THE SHOE FACTORY

I just couldn't stand the daily sole crushing

HOW DOES THE MOON CUT HIS HAIR?

Eclipse it

WHEN DOES A JOKE BECOME A DAD JOKE?

When it becomes apparent!

I COULDN'T FIGURE OUT HOW THE SEATBELT WORKED

but then it just clicked

WHY ARE BANK TELLERS GREAT AT YOGA?

They know how to find their balance!

WHY DID THE ROBOT GO TO THERAPY?

It had too many personal "i"-ssues

HOW DO YOU PROTECT A BAGEL?

Lox it up!

WHAT KIND OF COFFEE DOES A VAMPIRE DRINK??

De-coffin-ated!

WHY CAN'T YOU TELL A TACO A SECRET?

They tend to spill the beans!

DOGS CAN'T OPERATE MRI MACHINES

But cat scan

WHY DOES SNOOP DOGG ALWAYS CARRY AN UMBRELLA?

Fo' Drizzle

WHY ARE FROGS SO GOOD AT BASKETBALL?

They never miss a jump shot!

WHY DO PENGUINS LOVE TO CHAT?

Because they always have icebreakers!

WHERE ARE AVERAGE THINGS MANUFACTURED?

The Satisfactory

HOW CAN YOU TELL IT'S A DOGWOOD TREE?

From its bark!

WHAT BONE WILL A DOG NEVER EAT?

A trombone

WHY DID THE OCEAN BREAK UP WITH THE POND?

It thought the pond was too shallow!

WHERE DO BABY CATS LEARN TO SWIM?

The kitty pool

WHY DO PEPPERS MAKE GREAT DETECTIVES?

They always get jalapeño your business!

I HATE INSECTS PUNS

they really bug me

I PUT A NEW FREEZER NEXT TO THE REFRIGERATOR

now they're just chilling

MY NEW GIRLFRIEND WORKS AT THE ZOO

I think she's a keeper

I'M TAKING PART IN A STAIR CLIMBING COMPETITION

I need to step up my game!

I USED TO BUILD STAIRS FOR A LIVING

Business was up and down

MY THERAPIST SAYS I HAVE A PREOCCUPATION FOR REVENGE

We'll see about that

JUST RECEIVED A CARD FULL OF RICE

It's from Uncle Ben

LOCAL MAN KILLED BY FALLING PIANO

It will be a low key funeral

I SAW A DOCUMENTARY ON HOW SHIPS ARE KEPT TOGETHER

Riveting

CRIME IN MULTI-STORY CAR PARKS

That is wrong on so many different levels

AS A KID I WAS MADE TO WALK THE PLANK

We couldn't afford a dog

I'VE GIVEN UP ASKING RHETORICAL QUESTIONS

What's the point?

I'M LOOKING FOR THE GIRL NEXT DOOR TYPE

I'm just gonna keep moving house till I find her

I HAVE TWO BOYS, 5 AND 6

We're no good at naming things in our house

PEOPLE WHO USE SELFIE STICKS NEED TO HAVE A GOOD

long look at themselves

THE PROBLEM ISN'T THAT OBESITY RUNS IN YOUR FAMILY

It's that no one runs in your family

IF YOU'RE BEING CHASED BY A PACK OF TAXIDERMISTS

do not play dead

WHY DOES A BAKER ALWAYS KNOW WHERE HE'S GOING?

He's always heading yeastbound

WHAT'S THE DIFFERENCE BETWEEN A 'HIPPO' AND A 'ZIPPO'?

One is really heavy, the other is a little lighter

I WONDER HOW MANY CHAMELEONS

snuck onto the Ark

IF A PARSLEY FARMER GETS SUED

can they garnish his wages?

WHAT'S A FROG'S FAVORITE TYPE OF SHOES?

Open toad sandals

THEY SAY MONEY CAN'T BUY YOU HAPPINESS

Well... I just bought a happy meal

I'M ENTERING THE WORLDS TIGHTEST HAT COMPETITION

Just hope I can pull it off

WHAT KIND OF CAR DOES AN EGG DRIVE?

A Yolksvagen

DID YOU HEAR ABOUT THE CORDUROY PILLOW?

It's making headlines

TIME FLIES LIKE AN ARROW

Fruit flies like a banana

I WAS GOING TO TELL A CARPENTRY JOKE

but I couldn't find any of that woodwork

IF ATTACKED BY A MOB OF CLOWNS

go for the juggler

I SYMPATHIZE WITH BATTERIES

I'm not included in anything either

NOT ALL MATH PUNS ARE TERRIBLE

Just sum

I WAS JUST IN THE BREAKROOM

and someone threw milk at me... How dairy!

SOMETIMES I TELL FISH JOKES

just for the halibut

WHAT DO BIOLOGISTS WEAR TO WORK ON CASUAL FRIDAY?

Genes!

PIG PUNS

are so boaring

WHAT DID THE SUSHI SAY TO THE BEE?

Wasabi

DID YOU HEAR THAT LARRY GOT A NEW JOB WORKING FOR OLD MACDONALD'S?

He's the new CIEIO

WHY DO BIRDS SING EVERY MORNING?

They don't go to work

A DUNG BEETLE WALKS INTO A BAR AND ASKS

Is this stool open?

WHICH DAY DO POTATOES FEAR THE MOST?

Fryday

WHAT DO YOU GET WHEN YOU CROSS A CHICKEN WITH A FOX?

A fox

MY DOG USED TO CHASE PEOPLE ON A BIKE A LOT

It got so bad I had to take his bike away

WE HOPE YOU LOVED THE BOOK

PLEASE SHARE YOUR EXPERIENCE ON AMAZON!

We truly appreciate your support and feedback.

Thank you for helping our independent publishing company thrive, and we hope "No Pun Intended Too" continues to bring laughter and joy to you and those around you.

Wishing you endless chuckles and groans,

WILL LIVINGTON © COPYRIGHT 2023

www.ingramcontent.com/pod-product-compliance
Lightning Source LLC
Chambersburg PA
CBHW070438010526
44118CB00014B/2097